THE POWER OF RELATIONAL ACTION

Edward T. Chambers

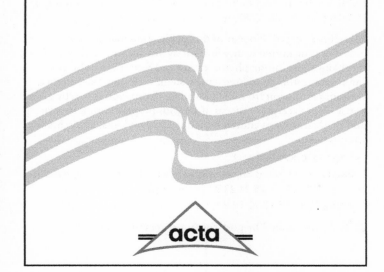

THE POWER OF RELATIONAL ACTION
by Edward T. Chambers

Edited by Gregory F. Augustine Pierce
Cover and text design and typesetting by Patricia Lynch

Copyright © 2009, 2017 by Edward T. Chambers

Published by ACTA Publications, 4848 N. Clark Street, Chicago, IL 60640, (800) 397-2282, www.actapublications.com

ISBN: 978-0-87946-392-2
Printed in the United States of America by Total Printing Systems
Year 30 29 28 27 26 25 24 23 22 21 20 19 18
Printing 15 14 13 12 11 10 9 8 7 6 5

♻ Text printed on 30% post-consumer recycled paper.

PUBLISHER'S NOTE

★★★★

Ed Chambers was a man of action. So trying to pry a book out of him, even a short one like this, was not easy.

On the other hand, few people had as much to say or as much experience to base it on as Chambers did, so whatever prying was necessary was worth the work. It was really a matter of getting him to stop mulling and start writing.

Here is the second booklet in his "Mulling About Acting in the World-As-It-Is" series. This one is on the power of "relational action," which is his phrase for the public one-to-one encounter between two human beings trying to size each other up.

Who should read this booklet? Anyone who wants to understand power and how it can be organized for the common good, anyone who wants to revitalize a church or synagogue or temple or mosque, anyone who wants to build a citizens organization.

You won't find a "how to" set of instructions here. You are more likely to discover a "why" and a "wherefore." You will, in effect, be reading over the shoulder of the founder of organizing as a profession as he "mulls" about what he has learned over the last fifty-five years as an agitator, mentor, trainer and executive director of the Industrial Areas Foundation.

When I asked Chambers who is audience was for this series of booklets, he told me he was writing them for himself. It wasn't so much that he didn't want to communicate with the reader. He just didn't want to have to adapt what he wanted to say to a particular group or use.

But in general, Chambers had in mind the next generation of leaders and organizers in the post-Obama era, one in which a former organizer of mixed race (who attended the IAF national training sessions before he got into politics) was twice elected president of the United States. In current political environment, what Ed Chambers had to tell us has even more urgency and relevance.

In the first booklet in this series, titled *The Body Trumps the Brain*, Chambers explores how people obtain what he calls "social knowledge," as opposed to academic knowledge. He shows that human beings learn with all their senses, including instinct and intuition, and not just with their mind. *The Power of Relational Action* takes that discussion the next step by looking at how humans should relate to one another and to the world.

In the third book in this series, titled *Action Creates Public Life*, Chambers argues that it is by taking action that we define who we are as adults and help create the world-as-it-should-be. It is written for those who want to participate in shaping society rather than sit around and complain about things.

If you want to read the mullings of a truly original thinker, you've come to the right place.

Gregory F. Augustine Pierce
President and Publisher
ACTA Publications

INTRODUCTION

★★★★

MULLING ABOUT ACTING IN THE WORLD-AS-IT-IS

mull: 1. to study or ruminate; ponder. 2. to think about carefully; consider.

Webster's Encyclopedic Unabridged Dictionary of the English Language

★★★★

In many people, spirit never gets developed, because they never connect with others in a real way. Capitalism tells us that the self is all-important, because it wants us to be isolated consumers, each making his or her own decisions, without being accountable to one another. Our educational system teaches self-sufficiency and independence, not community and interdependence. Political leaders want us as individual voters who can be reached one at a time by means of the mass media and the Internet. The health industry treats us all as patients, that is, people who wait "patient-ly" in isolation to be treated by the medical system. Even organized religion, which purports to be the most communal and relational of all human endeavors, really wants us to have a private, personal experience of God.

None of them are correct, of course. We cannot be successful—or even human—without other people. We can't grow or develop without the diversity offered by other viewpoints, other life experiences, other value systems. Some of us get this on a very limited basis in our private lives: We "fall in love" with another; we get married; we have kids; sometimes we make a good friend or two. This is often the extent of our relational lives. The rest is superficial, academic, and task-oriented.

> **We can't grow or develop without the diversity offered by other viewpoints, other life experiences, other value systems.**

This is the second booklet in the series "Mulling About Acting in the World-As-It-Is" that I am writing near the end of an active career trying to bring about social change in our society. It focuses on a simple question: Can we learn how to mix our human spirit with that of others in public life? The answer is not obvious, for much of what passes for relationship in the public arena is merely politeness and "getting along." We talk about sports or movies or politics, but we never get to the core of our lives—our passions, our sources of energy, our deepest self-interest, what makes us "tick" as human beings.

We have a word for this human trait. It is our "spirit," and all humans get it at birth. That spirit is not individual, it is relational, because that is the way we human beings were created. We exist because life itself is relational: It consists of ourselves, other selves and the world—all in constant relationship with one another.

This is a new insight for me, one that I want to explore. This booklet is just a beginning. What I hope to cover here is how we can mix our human spirits in public life to help create the organizations and institutions we need for a better world, the world-as-it-should-be.

Edward T. Chambers
Former Executive Director
Industrial Areas Foundation

THE POWER OF RELATIONAL ACTION

★★★★

"The dogmas of the quiet past are inadequate
to the stormy present. As our case is new,
so we must think anew and act anew."

Abraham Lincoln

★★★★

In my over fifty-five years of organizing with the Industrial Areas Foundation (IAF), I have learned that the authentic goal of public life is the development of real relationships in the public arena, what I call "the mixing of human spirits." One of the key methods I have used to do this is what we in the IAF refer to as "relational meetings" or "one-to-ones."

Relational meetings allow two people to expose each other to the deepest level of what they really care about and are willing to act upon. This offers them the opportunity to mix their spirits, and there is nothing more powerful in the world than this. That is why the disciplined practice of relational action is revolutionary and why the powers that be don't understand it. And that is why most people won't ever do "one-to-ones."

But for those who do them, we have the "power to become children of God" (John 1:12).

There are two ways to act in the world-as-it-is. One is task-oriented and the other is relational. Relational is more powerful, for it will eventually accomplish task, while the task-oriented approach often ignores or misses or minimizes the power of relationships.

The relational approach uses all the senses, while the task-oriented often remains in the brain. Relationships are the province of sex, love, emotion, and guts. Task comes from thinking too much.

> **Relationships are the province
> of sex, love, emotion, and guts.
> Task comes from thinking too much.**

The word *relationship* comes from the Latin verb *relatio*, which means "to tell," as in "to relate what happened" or "to tell the story." *Task* is from the Latin word *taxa*, which was the word for taxes but implies to "rate" or "value" something. So relationships are about "telling or making a story," while task is an intellectual accounting or cataloging of a particular work that needs to be done.

In the world of action, this is how this distinction plays itself out. Those who are eager to quantify things are drawn to task. Thus they are worried about how much they have accomplished in a particular amount of time or because of a certain amount of effort. They couldn't care less how these tasks are accomplished, and they don't worry about who does the tasks with them. Those who take a relational approach, on the other hand, are much more concerned with who is with them on a particular effort and the manner in which their joint action is carried out. A task-oriented person can be a loner. In fact, that is often preferable in terms of getting the work done. "I can do it easier and quicker myself," he or she might say. The relationally-oriented person is interested in power and organization, in how institutions get changed, in understanding who is calling the shots and for what purpose.

It's up to you to decide which kind of approach you are going to take in your life, but building relationships for action is ultimately more powerful, long-lasting, and satisfying than accomplishing a series of tasks. This booklet is about the power of relational action. It is about the mixing of human spirits. It is about duplicating the experience of birth in our public lives.

We'll die if we only have private life. While private life is where we experience the mixing of human spirits at the most fundamental level, we also need public life to get outside of ourselves, to leave our mark on the world, to fulfill our individual calling or specific vocation.

If you want to succeed in public life, however, there is one key skill, tool, technique that will ensure your success. But it comes at a high price. It is hard work that must be done on a disciplined basis over a long period of time; there is an extremely low initial rate of return; and you must both know yourself (what makes you tick), be interested in others (what makes them tick) and be willing to be vulnerable and accountable with others and enter into relationships with them that lead to action.

> **We need public life
> to get outside of ourselves,
> to leave our mark on the world,
> to fulfill our individual calling
> or specific vocation.**

This process is already being used by literally hundreds of organizers and leaders in community groups around the country, as well as by the most creative and productive people in business, politics, religion and the media.

It is a skill they don't teach in college or in corporate America, because it is revolutionary in its conception, its execution, and its results. If enough people actually learned and practiced it, we would change completely how we relate to one another and conduct our public lives.

I developed this tool over many years and with the help of many others. We in the IAF call it the "one-to-one, body-to-body, face-to-face relational meeting," or "one-to-one" for short. During my years of public life, I have conducted literally thousands of them, and I consider the development and teaching of the one-to-one relational meeting to be my greatest contribution to the human endeavor.

★★★★

I discovered the one-to-one meeting out of necessity when I was about twenty-five years old. I had just started working for Saul Alinsky and his Industrial Areas Foundation and was assigned to try to build a community organization in the predominately white but racially troubled South Side of Chicago. I had no day-to-day direction from Alinsky or anyone else, and I certainly had precious little experience myself.

So I started by meeting as many people as I could—primarily clergy and laypeople from the Protestant congregations in the area whose denominations were sponsoring the organizing effort. So I was even outside the comfort zone of my Roman Catholic upbringing. Plus I was a white guy from Clarion, Iowa, with little understanding of the kind of racial tension then prevalent in Chicago, which most sociologists considered the most segregated city in the United States at the time.

So I had to reflect on what the hell I was doing there. One thing I knew is that I could not start out by talking with strangers about the most obvious problem—the elephant in the room, if you will—which was racial injustice. I would have been ridden out of town on the proverbial rail if I had, and even as young and inexperienced as I was, I realized that I had to talk about something else. What was it?

I had no obvious leaders to start with. I would get a few names, meet with them, get a couple of names from them, meet with those people. This went on for about two years—a saturation of one-to-one meetings with people I didn't know and who not only didn't know me but also were suspicious of who I was and what my agenda might be.4

Somehow, over that two-year period, I began to realize that I needed to talk with people about themselves...and about me. I learned that the best meetings I was having were the ones where we didn't talk about the "problems" in the community but instead discussed our backgrounds and values and passions and vision. I got to know the people by asking them about themselves, by listening to their response, and by sharing with them a little bit about myself. The best meetings were "relational," in that they led to the beginnings of a possible relationship between myself and the people I was trying to organize. I also noticed that the best meetings were always done one-to-one and face-to-face—not in groups and certainly not over the telephone.

16

Thus began my understanding and development of the relational meeting. I recognized the genius of the one-to-one because that is where the heart came into the organizing process. I could feel when a person had real passion and conviction by how they talked about themselves and their families and community. I could tell by the stories they told what values they held dear and might be willing to act upon. And they could do the same about me.

I also noticed that the best meetings were always done one-to-one and face-to-face—not in groups and certainly not over the telephone.

The volume of the number of individual meetings I was doing and my stick-to-it-ness was what allowed me to put together my first real community organization, the Organization of the Southwest Community. We eventually had a founding convention of about 450 people representing 28 congregations and civic groups, and I remember that the very last delegation that walked in just before the gavel went down to call the meeting to order was a small group from a black Protestant church on the edge of the community's boundaries. Otherwise, the organization would have started out entirely white—not unusual for that place and time, but not what the community needed or wanted.

I was sweating that the one African-American delegation wasn't going to show up, but I was also trying to get the convention started on time. The black pastor and about five of his laypeople walked in at the last minute. We had them seated down front, so when they came in everyone saw them immediately. There was a feeling of shock and tension among most of the white delegates. They weren't expecting this, but nobody walked out or cat-called. I knew from the hundreds of relational meetings I had conducted that they wouldn't. Despite their fears and even prejudices, I knew that the people we had assembled had good values and were looking for solutions to the racial tensions in their area. I had appealed to their best—not their worst—instincts, and they knew what made me tick in the same way I knew what made them tick: We had done our relational meetings together.

So what are one-to-one relational meetings? They are the glue that brings people together and allows them to embrace the tension of living between the world-as-it-is and the world-as-it-should-be. Properly understood, the relational meeting is not a science, not a technique, but an art form in which one spirit goes after another spirit to create connection, confrontation, and an exchange of talent and energy, eventually leading to some kind of joint action. Perhaps one-to-ones would be better named "the mixing of human spirits."

The relational meeting is an encounter that is face-to-face and one-to-one. It's purpose is to explore the possibility of a public relationship with another person. Let me stop there. I said a public relationship. This may be one of the biggest causes of misunderstanding and failure regarding relational meetings. We are not looking for new "friends" when we are conducting a series of one-to-ones. Friendship is something that happens in private life. It usually happens accidentally (a roommate in college, a next-door neighbor, a co-worker), grows slowly over time, is based on many shared experiences, and often lasts a lifetime. Real friendships are few and far between. You are lucky if you have a handful in a lifetime. And, of course, one of those "friendships" can turn to romance, physical intimacy, and even marriage. And marriage can produce more private relationships in the form of children, grandchildren, in-laws, etc.

> **Properly understood, the relational meeting is an art form in which one spirit goes after another spirit to create connection, confrontation, and an exchange of talent and energy.**

None of that is what we are looking for in one-to-ones. The purpose of a systematic, disciplined, organized process of relational meetings is a public relationship—

one built on mutual self-interest, respect and power, that eventually leads to joint action. When you are doing one-to-ones, you are searching for energy, insight and a willingness to act and to lead. Where these are present, you will have found some additional strength and talent to add to your public collective, whether that be a citizens organization, a local religious congregation, a political party, or some kind of social movement. Without hundreds of such relational meetings, people cannot forge lasting public relationships that lead to collective action.

> **Without hundreds of such relational meetings, people cannot forge lasting public relationships that lead to collective action.**

For the relational meeting is a means to an end. The end is always collective action, and with that kind of power we can change the world.

James Madison said, "Great things can only be accomplished in a narrow compass." The relational meeting is that narrow compass—one person face-to-face with another—but significant in intention and purpose. A one-to-one is a small stage that lends itself to acts of memory, imagination and reflection. It constitutes a public conversation on a scale that allows space for thoughts, aspirations, values and talent to mix. It is where public newness begins, and it is the only hope for the long-term survival and triumph of democracy.

A solid relational meeting brings up stories that reveal people's deepest commitments and the experiences that give rise to their core values. In fact, the most important thing that happens in a good one-to-one is the telling of stories that open a window into the passions that animate people. In a relational meeting with one African-American leader, an organizer asked why she seemed so willing to take risks, why she was able to step up and lead when others held back. She seemed, by nature, to be a shy person, happier in her home and among her family members than in the public arena. But in response to the organizer's pointed question in the one-to-one meeting, the woman told the following story.

★★★★

When I was a young girl in North Carolina, my sister and I began to attend the local Roman Catholic church. In those days, blacks sat in the back pews. I was a very large young girl, rather heavy, and so was my sister. When we first went to that church, I saw no reason why my sister and I should sit in the back. So one Sunday we went right up and sat in the first pew. The pastors and ushers were upset. The pastor came over before Mass and asked me if we would please sit in the back, like all the other blacks. I was scared as I could be, but I just couldn't see where God would care where we sat, so I said no. Finally, the ushers came and carried me and my sister to the back. Carried us right down the aisle of the church.

On the next Sunday, my sister and I sat in the front pew again, and the priest and the ushers came and they hauled us off again, huffing and puffing. On the third Sunday, the same thing happened. By this time, we were pretty well known. Two black girls who got carried away to the back of the church every Sunday. My family, my mother particularly, was frightened at what we were doing, but she said we were doing the right thing.

On the fourth Sunday, the priest and ushers didn't do a thing. The Mass started, the choir sang, we took our seats in front, and from then on we sat where we wanted in that church and in any Roman Catholic church we ever attended.

This is the kind of story that you are looking for in every one-to-one: a story that is a window into a person's soul. After doing many relational meetings, every experienced leader and organizer hears stories like this. They also learn to tell these kind of stories about themselves. For it is the sharing of stories that sustain and energize the entire process. As philosopher Hannah Arendt said in her book *The Human Condition*, "The essence of who somebody is…can come into being only when life departs, leaving behind nothing but a story."

> **It is the sharing of stories that sustain and energize the entire process.**

★★★★

Is the technique of doing one-to-ones only applicable to organizing? I don't think so. In fact, I know that successful people in politics, business, religion and other work involving people do it all the time. I have read that Bill Clinton, when he was studying in England as a Rhodes Scholar, wouldn't go out drinking with his friends until after he had written out index cards on everyone that he had met that day. These cards became the basis for the "Friends of Bill" list that he used when he went into politics.

A good missionary who is sent into a new area does this as well. Rather than getting up in the pulpit and preaching at people right at the beginning, he or she goes around doing relational meetings. Only after these relationships have been started does the good missionary even think about starting to evangelize.

And if you want to understand how the top people in corporate America operate, you need only understand the relational meeting. Top business leaders spend most of their time doing one-to-ones with their own employees, with potential allies and colleagues, with industry analysts, and even with their competitors. What they are looking for are like-minded, talented people whom they can hire or ask to be on their board of directors.

> **If you want to understand how the top people in corporate America operate, you need only understand the relational meeting.**

Then why is it so difficult to teach and do one-to-ones? The first reason is that we are all brainwashed by our parents and school systems that the important thing in life is that we have a job and make lots of money, that security is the greatest value, that risk is to be avoided, and that we should be liked by everyone. Once we have bought into this philosophy, which is endorsed and promoted by advertisers and the media, then taking the time and effort to do relational meetings is silly. Why would we want to find out what makes other people tick, why would we want to determine if we might have things in common with others, why would we want to invest in possible relationships—many of which will never pan out—if we are going to operate as isolated individuals and act as consumers our entire lives? Only if we want to change the world for the better, only if we see others as connected and important to our having a meaningful public life, would we want to learn to do one-to-ones.

Let's face it: Most people are followers. It requires less energy to follow than to lead. We are taught to do what others want us to do and to follow our corporate and political and religious leaders. There is no need to think for ourselves. And if there is no need to think for ourselves, there is certainly no reason to do hundreds of relational meetings. Early on in life, with decent looks and a little charm, we can go a long way in public life by playing the game and following the "celebrities." If we want to be leaders, however, then it falls back on us to initiate and create—and we need others to help us do so. Thus we start to do one-to-ones. A prime example of this occurred in the Muslim-American community in Chicago both before and after the terrorist attacks of 9/11/2001.

In the late 1990s, I was helping to organize a new citizens power organization in the city and suburbs of Chicago. It dawned on me that we had no involvement by the Muslim community, which had quietly grown into a considerable new force in the area. (In fact, there were more Muslims than Jews, and Muslims were one of the fastest-growing groups in the metropolitan area.) The problem was that—like most Americans—I knew few

Muslims and had even fewer real relationships. Fortunately, I had a skill to do something about it, and I did.

I remembered that I had had one conversation with a gentle Muslim business leader named Talat Othman that had gone fairly well. So I checked with two other sources, and they confirmed that he was a key person in the Islamic community. So I called Mr. Othman for a one-to-one meeting. He agreed, and I traveled to his suburban Chicago office to meet him. On the way, I decided to take a risk: I would fold three relational meetings into the first one! By that I meant that I would go beyond what I would normally have done in a first or second relational meeting and discuss my organizational needs very frankly in the hope that they would meet his self-interests as well.

We were at the time only six months away from the founding convention of a potential new organization that would call itself United Power for Action and Justice. The organizers (Stephan Roberson, Cheri Andes, Josh Hoyt), the many leaders, and I had done thousands of one-to-ones with mainline and evangelical Protestants, liberal and conservative Catholics, conservative and reform Jews, labor unions, civic and neighborhood organizations, social service and health institutions, labor unions and business organizations, and just about every other group we could find. We had involved Latinos, African-Americans, Asian-Americans; middle-class and poor; north, west and south sides; city and suburban. We knew that the founding convention was going to be the most diverse group ever assembled in a political arena that functioned primarily *on the "divide-and-conquer" philosophy of the old Mayor Daley machine, now run by his son and other protégés in typical Chicago fashion. But we had zero Muslims, and I was not willing to move forward without them.*

We had zero Muslims, and I was not willing to move forward without them.

In our one-to-one relational meeting, Mr. Othman recognized my problem, but he also heard my values and my passion. And he saw, even if only faintly, the self-interest of the Muslim community in being part of this effort from the very beginning. He told me, "Mr. Chambers, you would have to go to the southwest suburbs of Chicago and meet with the leaders of our mosques there." He knew that was where the Muslim organizational strength in the region was centered, and he gave me the names of leaders of six mosques. He said that he would call them and tell them that I would be calling and urge them to meet with me. He took a big risk in doing this, and I will always remember him for his courage and faith in me.

I went to work. I had a series of meetings with the leaders of those mosques, which led to a delegation of some 220 Muslims from five key mosques at the United Power for Action and Justice founding convention in the fall of 1997. There were 10,000 people at that convention, but none were more important than those 220. In fact, I made sure that they were seated in some of the front rows of the convention.

Of course, this beginning led to other relational meetings with other Muslim-American leaders after the convention was over. That is why four years later, on September 11, 2001, United Power for Action and Justice was able to do something that no other organization in America was able to do.

Almost immediately after 9/11, the Muslim leaders inside United Power for Action and Justice began meeting with the non-Muslim leaders about how they could jointly respond in a significant way to the terrorist attack and the subsequent targeting of Muslim-Americans for hate crimes, discrimination and prejudice. They decided that what was need more than anything else was a very large and very public meeting that would both introduce the growing Muslim-American community to their Chicago-land neighbors and also begin the process of developing real, mutually respectful, public relationships between Muslims and non-Muslims in the Chicago area.

The vision was large: We would organize some 4000 people—half followers of Islam and the other half everyone else—to meet on Sunday, November 18, at Chicago's Navy Pier, one of the largest and most prestigious public spaces in Chicago. The event was called "Chicagoans and Islam," and it was one of the most successful actions I have ever observed, because it was completely based on the idea of relational action.

28

Why did people show up? They came for several reasons. They came because they were scared—on both sides. Nothing like 9/11 had ever happened on such a large scale in American history, and no one knew what was going to happen next. They came because they really did not know each other. Most of the non-Muslims at the meeting had never talked with a Muslim before, at least not about anything important. The Muslims came because they knew the history of immigrants in this country and specifically in Chicago, and they knew that immigrants had never really been welcomed. This would not only be an opportunity for the Muslims to introduce themselves to their new neighbors. It would also be a chance for their new neighbors to welcome them into the community.

> They came because they were scared.
> They came because they really
> did not know each other.

And finally, both sides came because they were organized and had relationships with one another. This meeting was not called by the governor or the mayor; they could never have pulled it off. It was called by an organization that had spent the previous four or five years building relationships, face-to-face and one-to-one. This meeting was not merely announced in the media hoping that people would just show up. It was organized through all the member institutions of United Power for Action and Justice. People showed up on buses. Four thousand people pledged they would come, and over 3900 of them showed up. There were no "incidents," because everyone who was there was there for the same reason: to meet people they did not know or understand.

Two thousand of them were Muslim, and two thousand were others from every ethnic background that makes up Chicago. Many of them were teenagers and young adults, encouraged to be there by their parents and clergy. The meeting was co-chaired by a Muslim businessman and a Catholic businessman. The highlight of the meeting came when a young Muslim woman and a young Christian woman conducted a relational meeting on the stage in front of the entire crowd. There is a famous photo of the two of them hugging, which ran on the front page of the Chicago Tribune the next morning. Immediately after the two young women finished, people were paired off in twos, one Muslim and one non-Muslim, to do a one-to-one on the floor of the convention hall. The sound and the energy of those 2000 relational meetings reverberated at Navy Pier and continues to do so throughout Chicagoland to this day.

★★★★

While the dominant culture tells us that cell phones, beepers, fax machines, e-mail and Internet chat rooms and blogs have made face-to-face, person-to-person communication obsolete, organizers and leaders who regularly do the intense work of relational meetings understand that these disciplined conversations touch our depths in a unique and irreplaceable way, even if one never sees the other person again. In relational meetings, the "why" questions so often avoided by people have a space in which to surface: Why are things like they are; why am I doing what I do; why don't I spend more time on the things I say are most important to me?

A relational meeting isn't selling or pushing an issue or membership or task in an organization or congregation. Those conducting a series of one-to-ones must listen rather than talk and ask questions rather than offer solutions. What is the other person thinking and feeling? What makes this person tick? What's his or her number-one priority? Our basic tools are our eyes, ears and feelings—as well as our instinct and intuition.

Short succinct questions are the best: "Why do you say that;" "what's that mean to you;" "why do you care;" "have you ever tried to do anything about it?" You must be prepared to interrupt with brief, tight questions like these, to then shut up and listen, and finally to share some things about yourself. Even as you are talking or listening, you need to be alert for the next question. The art of relational meetings has to do with this in-and-out movement. We are looking for interests, talents and connections across the spectrum of race, class, religion and politics. A one-to-one is an entry point to public life.

In casual meetings, we take people as they present themselves. We don't push or probe. We don't dig. We don't challenge where a notion came from.

> # A one-to-one
> ## is an entry point to public life.

Mixing human spirits has a certain form and requires certain skills to practice. Those of us who become practiced in the art of the relational meeting have learned to use our whole selves—body and spirit, charms and personality, compassion and wit, humor and anger—in short, intense, focused human encounters. When a good one-to-one occurs, two people connect in a way that transcends ordinary, everyday conversation. Both people have the opportunity to pause and reflect on their personal experience regarding the tension between the world-as-it-is and the world-as-it-should-be. At that moment, a new public relationship can be born, two human spirits can mix, and both people can gain power to be truer to their best selves, to live more effectively and creatively, to take action together for the common good.

A CLOSING MULLING

Why in Christian belief does God have three persons? Why did Christians come up with the Trinity to describe what God is like? It is because God is an infinite and eternal relationship: Father to Son, Son to Holy Spirit, Holy Spirit to Father.

In the Abrahamic traditions of Judaism, Christianity and Islam, humans are made in the *imago Dei*, the image and likeness of God, and as such we are infused with divinity itself. It is a gift we are all given at birth. We have a spiritual inclination to interact with others and with the world, to reach out, to change, to correct, to build, to create, to procreate, to exercise power.

We humans are composed of three drives, just like the Godhead. This is a recent revelation for me. With this relational power and mix inside of us, with divine power grounded in us, why don't we act more, make changes more often, relate more effectively, and start transforming the world?

We create the world-as-it-should-be when we organize these three together:

OURSELF   OTHER SELVES   THE WORLD.

REFLECTING WITH SCRIPTURE
ON COMMUNITY ORGANIZING
by Rev. Jeff Krehbiel
The former pastor of the Church of the Pilgrims in Washington,
D.C., and co-chair of the Washington Interfaith Network offers
reflections on four passages from Scripture and how they relate to
the experience of community organizing. He also offers a Group
Study Guide for congregational use. 60 pages, paperback

EFFECTIVE ORGANIZING
FOR CONGREGATIONAL RENEWAL
by Michael Gecan
The author of *Going Public* and co-executive director of the
Industrial Areas Foundation describes how the tools of organizing
can and are transforming Protestant, Catholic, Jewish and Muslim
congregations. Included are five case studies of congregations that
have used this process to grow. 54 pages, paperback

REBUILDING OUR INSTITUTIONS
by Ernesto Cortes, Jr.
Ernie Cortes, the co-executive director of the Industrial Areas
Foundation, argues that community organizing cultivates the
practices needed for democracy to thrive, including one-on-one
relational meetings, house meetings, and systematic reflection
on them afterwards. This book contains several examples from
organizations in California, Louisiana, and Texas that helped
local congregations and other mediating institutions identify,
confront, and change things that were destroying their families
and communities. 30 pages, paperback